KÖNEMANN

— MAKING PASTA —

Pasta comes in a great variety of shapes and sizes

Pasta and noodles have been enjoyed in many forms throughout Europe and Asia for centuries.

Versatile, quick, and easy-to-prepare, pasta is also inexpensive. Served simply with butter and cheese or dressed with the most elaborate sauce – pasta can be right for any occasion.

The recipes included in this book mainly use dried pasta, which is both quick and convenient. For a delicious change, try substituting fresh pasta.

THE DOUGH

Pasta dough is simple to prepare. Different flavors and textures can be achieved by altering the basic ingredients just a little.

Pasta dough should have a rather dry texture and be quite firm. If the dough becomes too moist, it is difficult to work with. If this happens, knead in a little extra flour to achieve the right consistency.

Kneading is essential to make the dough elastic and easy to handle. Check dough after 5 to 10 minutes of kneading. It is sufficiently kneaded when you make a light indentation in it with your finger and the dough springs back immediately. At this stage, the dough is too elastic to roll, so wrap it in plastic wrap and let stand 10 minutes—the dough will relax and be easier to roll out.

Fresh Pasta Dough

Preparation time:
  10 minutes
Cooking time: None

3 cups all-purpose flour
3 eggs
3 tablespoons water
1 tablespoon olive oil

1 In a large mixing bowl or on a flat surface place flour; make a well in the center. In a small bowl whisk together eggs, water, and oil.
2 Add 3/4 of egg mixture to flour, mixing well with two table knives. Add remaining egg mixture, if necessary, to form a stiff dough.
3 Knead dough on a floured surface about 10 minutes or till smooth and elastic. Divide dough into four portions. Use as directed in the recipes.

1 Place flour on a flat surface; make well in the center. Add egg mixture.

2 Mix dough using two flat-bladed knives.

3 Knead dough until smooth and elastic.

Pasta varieties, from left: Wheatgerm and Garlic, Cheese and Basil, Lemon and Pepper, Spinach, Almond, Saffron, Buckwheat, Tomato, and Wholewheat Pastas.

Fresh Semolina Pasta

Preparation time:
   10 minutes
Cooking time: None

3 cups fine semolina or
   durum wheat
2 eggs
3/4 cup lukewarm water
1 tablespoon olive oil

1 In a large mixing bowl place semolina; make a well in the center. In a small bowl whisk together eggs, water, and oil.
2 Add 3/4 of the egg mixture to the flour, mixing with two table knives till well combined. Add remaining egg mixture, if necessary, to form a stiff dough.
3 Knead dough on a floured surface about 10 minutes or till smooth and elastic. Divide dough into four portions. Use as directed in the recipes.

ROLLING PASTA

Pasta can be rolled by hand, which takes a little time. It is easier to manage if the pasta is rolled in small portions.

Using a pasta machine makes rolling the pasta much easier. If you have a passion for making fresh pasta often, it is a worthwhile investment.

Rolling by Hand
Take 1/4 of the dough and place it on a lightly floured surface. Flatten dough lightly with the palm of your hand.
   Using a large rolling pin, roll pasta out thinly, rolling from the center to the edge. Avoid rolling over the edge since this makes it paper thin and harder to handle. Keep moving

rolled dough and dust surface and rolling pin with flour occasionally.

After rolling, cut and shape as desired. If the pasta is not being cut or shaped immediately, cover with a clean damp towel. This prevents the dough from drying out.

Rolling by Machine
Divide dough into four portions and flatten lightly on a floured surface.

Set roller on the pasta machine to the widest setting and dust with a little flour.

Feed each portion of dough through the machine twice. Lay dough flat on a lightly floured surface and fold into thirds. Feed the folded pasta, unfolded edge first, through the machine. Feed the pasta through the machine 6 more times till it becomes smooth and silky. If pasta sticks, dust lightly with flour.

Change setting on machine to bring rollers one notch closer together. Feed pasta through once only – this will make it thinner and longer. Set machine one notch closer together again and feed pasta through. Repeat this process till the machine is set on the second thinnest setting. At this stage the pasta is the ideal thickness for most uses. If you prefer finer pasta, then roll pasta through the thinnest setting. Cut or shape as desired.

CUTTING PASTA
Ribbon-shaped Noodles
Roll sheets of pasta jelly-roll style to form a long cylinder. Slice into desired widths. Unravel and cook right away or allow to dry in an airy spot before storing. If pasta is a little too moist, dust it lightly with flour before rolling. Rolled pasta can be fed through the cutters of a

Rolling Pasta by Hand

1 Place dough on a floured surface and roll from the center towards the edges.

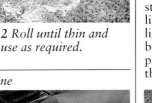

2 Roll until thin and use as required.

Rolling Pasta with a Machine

1 Feed flattened dough through rollers.

2 Fold pasta into thirds.

3 Feed pasta again through rollers, reducing width until thin.

pasta machine to form long ribbons.

Lasagna or Cannelloni
Use a sharp, straight-edged knife or sharp fluted pastry wheel. Cut lasagna into the same size as your baking dish or into 10 x 2½-inch strips. Cut cannelloni into 5 x 4-inch sheets. Then boil and cool them before filling and rolling.

Bows and Twists
To make bows, cut rolled pasta into 1½-inch squares with a fluted pastry wheel. Pinch middle together to form bows.
To make twists, cut pasta into 2 x ¾-inch strips with a fluted pastry wheel. Cut a ¾-inch slit down the top half of the strip. Pull bottom half up through cut to form a twist.

Filled Pasta
To make tortellini, cut pasta into 2-inch circles. Place a little filling on one side of the circle and lightly brush other half with water. Join edges together and press firmly to form a crescent shape. Curve the crescent around and join tips together, sealing with a little water.
To make ravioli, place a sheet of rolled pasta onto a flat surface. Spoon mounds of filling across the width and down the length of the pasta at 1½-inch intervals. Lightly brush between mounds with a little water. Lay a second sheet of pasta on top of the first layer. Press firmly between the mounds. Cut between mounds into squares using a sharp knife or sharp fluted pastry wheel.

DRYING PASTA
Fresh pasta can be cooked as soon as it is made. However, if it is dried sufficiently, fresh pasta can be stored at room temperature indefinitely.
To dry pasta shapes, place on a flat tray or wire rack lined with paper towels. Place in a dry, airy spot. Turn regularly till crisp and thoroughly dry.
To dry ribbon-shaped noodles, either place loose nests of pasta on a wire rack and leave to dry or hang pasta over clean hangers or a clean broom handle or curtain rod suspended between two chairs. Let dry.
After pasta is thoroughly dried, store in an airtight container until ready to use.
Commercial dried pasta is always readily available. It is worth

Cutting Pasta

1 Roll up pasta jelly-roll style.

2 Cut pasta into ribbons with a sharp knife.

3 Or, feed rolled pasta through cutting section of pasta machine.

Shaping Tortellini

1 *Cut the rolled dough into circles.*

2 *Spoon a little filling on one side of circle.*

3 *Moisten other side and fold over to form a crescent.*

4 *Curve crescent around and join tips together. Seal with water.*

trying a few different brands until you find the one you like best. Brands of pasta vary slightly in texture and the time they take to cook.

COOKING PASTA

Pasta needs to be cooked properly before serving.

Fresh Plain Pasta
Cook in a large amount of boiling water. Traditionally, salt is added to the cooking water but this is not necessary if you are watching your sodium intake. For a sweet treat, pasta can be deep-fried and dusted with powdered sugar.

To cook pasta, bring a large pot of water to a rapid boil. Add a little oil to prevent sticking. Add pasta and give it a stir to ensure that it hasn't stuck to the bottom of the pan. Boil, uncovered, till pasta is al dente – firm, yet tender. Drain well in a colander.

To reheat cooked pasta, place in a dish over a saucepan of simmering water for about 10 minutes or till heated through.

Other Types of Pasta
Instant or precooked lasagna noodles can save you time since you don't need to cook the pasta before layering it in the baking dish with the other ingredients. Be sure to follow the package directions before using.

Pastas that contain a filling, such as ravioli or tortellini, are best purchased fresh or frozen. Fresh ravioli and tortellini usually need to be boiled for 5 to 7 minutes or till al dente. If pasta is frozen, allow about 10 to 12 minutes for cooking. Be sure to read and follow the package directions when cooking fresh or dried pasta.

FLAVORED PASTAS

You can add interest and variety to your pasta dishes by substituting fresh flavored pasta for the commercial dry varieties. The possibilities are endless and it is worth trying a few different combinations.

Tomato Pasta
Add 1 tablespoon tomato paste and 1 clove crushed garlic to egg mixture. This pasta is a lovely rich orange color which lightens a little when cooked.

Cheese and Basil Pasta
Add 1/2 cup grated Parmesan cheese and 2 tablespoons finely chopped fresh basil to flour before mixing with egg. This is delicious tossed with a little butter.

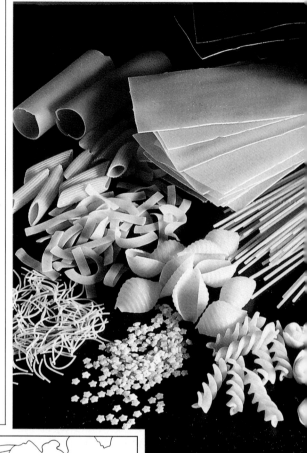

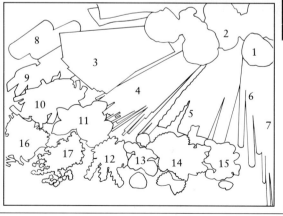

1. *Fettuccine*
2. *Vermicelli*
3. *Lasagne*
4. *Spaghetti*
5. *Pappardelle*
6. *Rigatoni*
7. *Bucatini*
8. *Cannelloni*
9. *Penne*
10. *Tagliatelle*
11. *Shells*
12. *Fusilli*

13. *Tortellini*
14. *Farfalle*
15.*Macaroni*
16. *Gramigna*
17. *Stellette*

Wheatgerm and Garlic Pasta
Replace 1/2 all-purpose flour with 1/2 cup wheatgerm and add 1/2 teaspoon garlic powder. Best served simply with a little olive oil and chopped fresh herbs.

Lemon and Pepper Pasta
Add 2 teaspoons finely shredded lemon peel and 1 teaspoon coarsely cracked pepper to flour before adding eggs. Delicious for seafood-filled tortellini or tossed with a light cream sauce.

Spinach Pasta
Cook 8 ounces fresh spinach leaves till tender; drain well. Finely chop and squeeze out excess moisture to make spinach quite dry. Add to flour before adding enough egg and oil to form a dough. This beautiful green pasta is perfect for spinach lasagna or with roasted meat.

Wholewheat Pasta
You can use all wholewheat flour, however, this will make a very heavy dough. It is best to use half whole wheat flour and half all-purpose flour. The pasta may need a little extra liquid. If so, add chilled water. This pasta has a delicious nutty flavor and slightly heavy texture.

Buckwheat Pasta
Replace 1 1/2 cups of the all-purpose flour with 1 1/2 cups buckwheat flour.

Almond Pasta
Combine 1 cup wholewheat flour, 3 1/2 ounces ground almonds, and 2 tablespoons powdered sugar. Add 2 eggs and 1/4 teaspoon almond extract and mix to form a dough.

— ESSENTIAL SAUCES —

Pasta is generally named after the shape, not the ingredients it contains. While some shaped pastas are more suited to particular styles of dishes, you shouldn't allow this to restrict you. Try different shapes for your favorite dishes and combine with any of these delicious sauces.

Rich Meat Sauce

Preparation time:
  15 minutes
Cooking time:
  1¹/2 hours
Makes about 6 cups

3 pounds ground round
  or sirloin
3 large onions,
  chopped
3 large green bell
  peppers, chopped
6 large cloves garlic,
  crushed
14¹/2-ounce can whole
  tomatoes
3 cups tomato purée
3 x 6-ounce cans
  tomato paste
1¹/2 cups dry red wine
¹/4 cup beef broth
1 tablespoon dried
  oregano, crushed
1 tablespoon dried
  basil, crushed
¹/2 teaspoon pepper

1 In a Dutch oven cook
ground round or
sirloin, onions, bell
peppers, and garlic till
meat is brown and
onion is tender.
Drain off fat.
2 Add undrained
tomatoes, tomato
purée, tomato paste, red
wine, beef broth,
oregano, basil, and
pepper. Bring to a boil;
reduce heat. Simmer,
uncovered, about
1¹/2 hours or till desired
consistency. Serve over
hot cooked pasta.

Anchovy and Garlic Sauce

Preparation time:
  8 minutes
Cooking time:
  5 minutes
Makes about 1 cup

¹/2 cup butter or
  margarine
4 cloves garlic, crushed
2 x 2-ounce cans
  anchovy fillets
2 to 4 tablespoons hot
  water
1 cup chopped parsley
Freshly ground pepper

1 In a small skillet melt
butter or margarine.
Add garlic and cook till
tender.
2 Drain anchovies,
reserving oil. Coarsely
chop. Stir anchovies
and reserved oil into

garlic mixture. Add
water and stir till well
combined. Heat
through.
3 Add parsley and
season with pepper.
Serve over hot cooked
pasta.

HINT
The salty flavor of
anchovies can be
mellowed by soaking
them in a little milk
for 30 minutes
before using. Drain
and use as directed
in recipe.

Tuna Sauce

Preparation time:
  10 minutes
Cooking time:
  15 minutes
Makes about 2 cups

¹/3 cup butter or
  margarine
1 clove garlic, crushed
8 ounces small
  mushrooms, thickly
  sliced
1 cup tomato purée
6¹/2-ounce can tuna,
  drained and flaked
Freshly ground pepper
Chopped parsley

1 In a saucepan melt
butter or margarine.
Add garlic and cook for
2 minutes. Remove
garlic from pan. Add
mushrooms and cook

over low heat till just softened.
2 Stir in tomato purée and tuna. Season with pepper. Cook over low heat for 10 minutes. Serve over hot cooked pasta and sprinkle with parsley.

Mushroom Cream Sauce

Preparation time:
  10 minutes
Cooking time:
  8 minutes
Makes about 2 cups

1/4 cup butter or margarine,
6 ounces small mushrooms, sliced
1 clove garlic, crushed
1 1/4 cups heavy cream
1 teaspoon finely shredded lemon peel
Pinch pepper
Pinch nutmeg
1/4 cup grated Parmesan cheese

1 In a saucepan melt butter or margarine. Add mushrooms and garlic and cook for 30 seconds. Stir in cream, lemon peel, pepper, and nutmeg.
2 Cook and stir over low heat for 1 to 2 minutes. Add Parmesan cheese and cook over low heat for 3 minutes. Serve over hot cooked pasta.

Fresh Tomato Sauce

Preparation time:
  15 minutes
Cooking time:
  45 minutes
Makes about 4 cups

1 tablespoon cooking oil
2 large onions, chopped
1/2 cup chopped celery
2 cloves garlic, crushed
4 cups chopped peeled tomatoes
1 teaspoon sugar
1/2 teaspoon dried oregano, crushed
1 bay leaf
Freshly ground pepper

1 In a saucepan heat oil. Cook onions, celery, and garlic over low heat till softened. Add tomatoes, sugar, oregano, bay leaf, and pepper.
2 Bring to a boil; reduce heat. Cover and simmer for 40 minutes. Remove bay leaf and toss with hot cooked pasta.

Variation: If you wish, add 4 ounces small mushrooms after cooking sauce 30 minutes. Cook 10 minutes more. Mushrooms can be sliced, quartered, or cooked in a little butter before adding to sauce.

Pesto

Preparation time:
  10 minutes
Cooking time:
  None
Makes 1 1/2 cups

4 ounces Parmesan, Romano, or pecorino cheese, cut into small cubes
1 cup tightly packed fresh basil leaves
1/2 cup pine nuts or walnuts
2 cloves garlic
1/2 cup olive oil

1 In a food processor place cheese cubes. Cover and process till finely grated. Add basil, nuts, and garlic. Cover and process till finely chopped.
2 With machine running, slowly pour in oil, processing till thickened and well combined. Toss with hot cooked pasta.

> ### HINT
> Pesto is best made fresh when required. Since fresh basil may not be available all year round, pesto can be made using all flat leaf parsley which will give you a different, yet delicious, sauce.

Clockwise from top left: Mushroom Cream Sauce, Fresh Tomato Sauce, and Pesto

— HEARTY FAMILY MEALS —

Tagliatelle con Prosciutto

See just how versatile pasta can be – there are so many delicious ways to combine pasta with fresh meat, chicken, and items from a delicatessen. The recipes here can provide many memorable meals that will convert even the fussiest eater to the delights of pasta.

These pasta dishes are examples of both European and Oriental cuisine, and most are quick and easy to prepare. Try one the next time you want a deliciously different meal.

Tagliatelle con Prosciutto

Preparation time:
   15 minutes
Cooking time:
   20 minutes
Serves 2

6 ounces tagliatelle
1/4 cup butter or
   margarine
1 onion, sliced
1 cup dry white wine
1/4 cup water
1 teaspoon beef
   bouillon granules
2 ounces prosciutto,
   coarsely chopped
1/2 a 10-ounce package
   frozen peas
2 tablespoons grated
   Parmesan cheese

1 Cook tagliatelle according to package directions or for 6 to 8 minutes or till al dente. Drain. Keep warm.
2 In a large saucepan melt butter or margarine. Add onion and cook till tender. Add wine, water, and bouillon granules. Cook, uncovered, for 5 to 8 minutes or till liquid evaporates. Add prosciutto and peas and cook for 2 minutes.
3 Add drained pasta to prosciutto mixture, tossing to coat. Sprinkle with Parmesan cheese.

Hint
To vary this dish, you can omit water and add 1/2 cup heavy cream at the end of cooking; heat through.

Spicy Tagliatelle

Preparation time:
   15 minutes
Cooking time:
   25 minutes
Serves 6

8 ounces green
   tagliatelle
8 ounces plain
   tagliatelle

Sauce
2 tablespoons butter or
   margarine
1 onion, chopped
4 ounces pepperoni or
   salami, chopped
4 ounces mushrooms,
   sliced
1/2 red bell pepper, cut
   into thin strips
1/4 cup dry white wine
3 tablespoons lemon
   juice
14 1/2-ounce can
   chopped tomatoes
1/4 cup grated Parmesan
   cheese
2 tablespoons chopped
   parsley

1 Cook tagliatelle according to package directions or for 6 to 8 minutes or till al dente. Drain. Keep warm.
2 For sauce, in a large skillet melt butter or margarine. Add onion and cook till tender. Add pepperoni or salami, mushrooms, and bell pepper. Cook for 2 minutes. Stir in wine and lemon juice. Add tomatoes. Bring to a boil; reduce heat. Simmer, uncovered, for 5 minutes.
3 Add pasta to skillet. Add Parmesan cheese and parsley, tossing to coat. Serve immediately.

Oriental Beef and Noodles

Preparation time:
  25 minutes
Cooking time:
  30 minutes
Serves 4

1/4 cup cooking oil

1 pound lean boneless beef, cut into 3/4-inch cubes
1 onion, chopped
1 clove garlic, crushed
14 1/2-ounce can tomatoes, drained
1/2 cup beef broth
2 tablespoons soy sauce
1/2 teaspoon finely chopped gingerroot

1 green bell pepper, cut into short strips
1 tablespoon cornstarch
2 tablespoons water
1 pound fettuccine

1 In a large skillet heat oil over medium-high heat. Add meat, a little at a time, to hot oil and cook till brown. Remove from skillet.

Oriental Beef and Noodles (top) and Stir-Fried Chicken (bottom)

2 Add onion and garlic to skillet and cook till tender. Add drained tomatoes and cook for 5 minutes, pressing tomatoes down with the back of a spoon.
3 Return beef to skillet. Stir in beef broth, soy sauce, and gingerroot. Cover and simmer about 20 minutes or till meat is tender. Add bell pepper and cook for 5 minutes more.
4 Stir cornstarch into water; add to skillet. Cook and stir till thickened and bubbly. Cook and stir 2 minutes more.
5 Meanwhile, cook fettuccine according to package directions or for 8 to 10 minutes or till al dente. Drain. Keep warm.
6 Place warm pasta on a serving platter. Spoon beef mixture over pasta.

> **HINT**
> Store fresh gingerroot in a jar with dry sherry. Slice off what you need and return the rest to the sherry. Cover and store for several weeks in the refrigerator.

Stir-Fried Chicken

Preparation time:
  25 minutes
Cooking time:
  20 minutes
Serves 4

10 ounces Chinese
  noodles
2 tablespoons cooking
  oil
1 pound boneless
  skinless chicken, cut
  into 1/2-inch thick
  strips
2 thin slices peeled
  gingerroot
Dash bottled hot
  pepper sauce
4 cups assorted cut up
  vegetables (carrots,
  tomatoes, broccoli,
  green beans,
  snow peas, or
  cabbage)
1 cup chicken broth
4 shallots, cut into
  2-inch pieces
2 tablespoons soy
  sauce
2 tablespoons dry
  sherry or vermouth
2 tablespoons
  cornstarch
8-ounce can sliced
  water chestnuts

1 Cook Chinese noodles according to package directions or for 3 to 5 minutes or till al dente. Drain. Keep warm.
2 Heat a large skillet over high heat. Add oil.

Stir-fry chicken, gingerroot, and pepper sauce for 2 to 3 minutes or till chicken is tender and no longer pink. Remove from skillet with a slotted spoon. Discard gingerroot.
3 Stir-fry assorted vegetables for 3 minutes. Add chicken broth and cook for 3 minutes more. Return chicken to skillet. Add shallots and cook for 1 minute.
4 Stir together soy sauce, sherry or vermouth, and cornstarch. Add to skillet with water chestnuts. Cook and stir till thickened and bubbly. Cook and stir for 2 minutes more.
5 Place noodles in a serving bowl. Spoon chicken mixture over noodles.

> **HINT**
> To remove the papery coating from a garlic clove, crush the clove with the flat side of a chef's knife and peel away the papery coating.

Spaghetti and Meatballs

Preparation time:
  25 minutes
Cooking time:
  50 minutes
Serves 6

Sauce
1 tablespoon cooking oil

1 small onion,
  chopped
14¹/2-ounce can
  chopped tomatoes
¹/2 cup water
¹/2 cup dry red
  wine
¹/4 cup tomato
  paste
1 small clove garlic,
  crushed
1 bay leaf
Pinch pepper

Meatballs
1 cup soft bread
  crumbs
¹/2 cup milk
1 pound lean ground
  beef
1 small onion, finely
  chopped
1 egg, beaten
1 tablespoon grated
  Parmesan cheese
1 tablespoon chopped
  fresh parsley

Spaghetti and Meatballs

18

¹/4 teaspoon dried
  oregano, crushed
Pinch pepper
3 tablespoons cooking
  oil
1 pound spaghetti
Grated Parmesan
  cheese

1 For sauce, in a large skillet heat 1 tablespoon oil. Cook onion in oil till tender. Add undrained tomatoes, water, red wine, tomato paste, garlic, bay leaf, and pepper. Bring to a boil; reduce heat. Simmer, uncovered, 20 minutes or till thickened, stirring occasionally.
2 For meatballs, combine bread crumbs and milk; let stand 5 minutes. Add ground beef, onion, egg, Parmesan cheese, parsley, oregano, and pepper. Mix till well combined. Shape meat mixture into balls.
3 In a skillet heat 3 tablespoons oil. Brown meatballs on all sides in hot oil. Drain. Transfer meatballs to sauce. Simmer, uncovered, for 15 minutes. Remove bay leaf.
4 Cook spaghetti according to package directions or 10 to 12 minutes or till al dente. Drain. Spoon meatballs and sauce over spaghetti. Serve with Parmesan cheese.

Chili Pork and Penne

Chili Pork and Penne

Preparation time:
  15 minutes
Cooking time:
  35 minutes
Serves 4

Sauce
4 ounces bacon, halved
  crosswise
1 onion, chopped
2 cloves garlic, crushed
1 14¹/2-ounce can
  chopped tomatoes
¹/2 fresh chili, seeded
  and finely chopped or
  ¹/4 to ¹/2 teaspoon
  ground red pepper
12 ounces penne
  pasta

Grated Parmesan
  cheese

1 For sauce, in a skillet cook bacon till cooked but not crisp. Drain off all but 1 tablespoon fat. Add onion and garlic and cook till onion is tender. Add undrained tomatoes and fresh chili or ground red pepper. Bring to a boil; reduce heat. Simmer, uncovered, for 15 to 20 minutes or till desired consistency.
2 Meanwhile, cook pasta according to package directions or for 14 minutes or till al dente. Drain. Spoon sauce over pasta. Serve with Parmesan cheese.

Beef and Rigatoni (left) and Pasta and Quick Meat Sauce (right)

Beef and Rigatoni

Preparation time:
  25 minutes
Cooking time:
  1 hour
Serves 6

2 tablespoons
  cooking oil
1¹/2 pounds round
  steak, cut into ³/4-inch
  cubes
2 onions, sliced
1 clove garlic,
  crushed
2 sprigs fresh parsley
1 sprig fresh thyme
1 bay leaf

1 cup beef broth
1 cup tomato purée or
  juice
2 carrots, sliced
Pinch pepper
8 ounces rigatoni
Chopped fresh
  parsley

1 In a large saucepan heat oil. Add meat and cook till brown. Add onions and garlic and cook till onions are tender. Pour off fat.
2 Tie together parsley, thyme, and bay leaf. Add ¹/4 cup of the beef broth and herb bundle to saucepan. Cover and simmer for 30 minutes. Add remaining stock, tomato purée or juice, carrots, and pepper. Cover and simmer for 30 minutes more. Remove herb bundle.
3 Meanwhile, cook pasta according to package directions or for 15 minutes or till al dente. Drain. Spoon sauce over pasta. Sprinkle with chopped parsley.

HINT
Partially frozen meat is much easier to cut into slices or cubes than defrosted or fresh meat.

Pasta and Quick Meat Sauce

Preparation time:
  15 minutes
Cooking time:
  45 minutes
Serves 4

Sauce
1 pound lean ground
  beef
1 small onion, chopped
1 clove garlic, crushed
2 cups water
6-ounce can tomato
  paste
1½-ounce package
  spaghetti sauce mix
½ teaspoon dried
  oregano, crushed
Pinch pepper
12 ounces spaghetti
Grated Parmesan
  cheese

1 For sauce, in a saucepan cook meat, onion, and garlic till meat is brown and onion is tender. Drain off fat.
2 Stir in water, tomato paste, spaghetti mix, oregano, and pepper. Bring to a boil; reduce heat. Cover and simmer for 15 minutes. Uncover and simmer for 8 to 10 minutes more.
3 Cook pasta according to package directions or for 10 to 12 minutes or till al dente. Drain. Spoon sauce over pasta. Serve with Parmesan cheese.

Beef Hotpot

Preparation time:
  15 minutes
Cooking time:
  40 minutes
Serves 6

1½ pounds lean
  ground beef
1 small onion, finely
  chopped
14½-ounce can
  chopped tomatoes
8 ounces mushrooms,
  sliced
2 stalks celery,
  sliced
2 tablespoons tomato
  paste
1 teaspoon dried basil,
  crushed
Pinch pepper
1½ cups water
1 small green bell
  pepper, cut
  into short, wide
  strips
1 small red bell pepper,
  cut into short, wide
  strips
1 pound penne
  pasta
¼ cup grated Parmesan
  cheese

1 In a large skillet cook ground beef and onion till meat is brown and onion is tender. Drain off fat. Stir in tomatoes, mushrooms, celery, tomato paste, basil, and pepper. Cover and simmer for 20 minutes. Stir in water and bell peppers. Simmer, uncovered, till desired consistency.
2 Meanwhile, cook pasta according to package directions or for 14 minutes or till al dente. Drain. Spoon beef mixture over pasta. Serve with Parmesan cheese.

Beef Hotpot

Burmese Noodles

Burmese Noodles

Preparation time:
  30 minutes
Cooking time:
  20 minutes
Serves 4

10 ounces Chinese noodles
Boiling water
8 ounces boneless skinless chicken breasts
3 tablespoons cooking oil
2 onions, sliced
2 cups shredded Chinese cabbage

1 stalk celery, thinly sliced
3 cloves garlic, crushed
2 tablespoons soy sauce
1 pound prawns or large shrimp, peeled and deveined
Pinch pepper

1 Place noodles in a bowl. Pour enough

boiling water over noodles to cover; let stand 10 minutes. Drop noodles in boiling water and cook for 3 minutes or till al dente. Drain. Line a wire rack with 2 layers of paper towels. Spread cooked noodles over paper towels.

2 Cut chicken into short strips. Preheat a wok or large skillet over high heat. Add oil. Stir-fry chicken for 2 to 3 minutes or till tender and no longer pink. Remove from wok or skillet. Add onions, cabbage, celery, garlic, and soy sauce and stir-fry for 3 to 4 minutes. Add prawns or shrimp and stir-fry 2 minutes or till tender.

3 Add cooked noodles to wok or skillet with shrimp mixture, tossing gently to combine. Heat through. Remove to a warm platter.

HINTS

☐ Bean sprouts, snow peas, and diced ham are great additions to Burmese Noodles.

☐ Sometimes this dish is garnished with scrambled eggs. When ready to serve, scramble 2 to 3 eggs till firm and cut into strips; scatter over noodles.

Spicy Pasta

Preparation time:
  20 minutes
Cooking time:
  20 minutes
Serves 6

1 pound penne pasta

Sauce
1 tablespoon cooking oil
1 large onion, sliced
*1 clove garlic,
  crushed*
*2 cups sliced kielbasa or
  Polish sausage*
*4 ounces mushrooms,
  sliced*
*14 1/2-ounce can
  chopped tomatoes*
*14-ounce can artichoke
  hearts, drained and
  halved*
*10 pitted ripe olives,
  sliced*
*2 teaspoons chopped
  fresh chilies*

*1/2 teaspoon dried basil,
  crushed*
Pinch pepper
*Shredded Parmesan
  cheese*

1 Cook pasta according to package directions or for 14 minutes or till al dente. Drain. Keep warm.

2 Meanwhile, for sauce, in a large skillet heat oil. Cook onion and garlic in oil till tender. Add kielbasa or sausage and mushrooms. Cook for 5 minutes. Stir in undrained tomatoes, artichoke hearts, olives, chilies, basil, and pepper.

3 Bring to a boil; reduce heat. Simmer, uncovered, till heated through. Add a little water or red wine if mixture becomes dry.

4 Place pasta on a serving plate. Spoon sauce over. Sprinkle with Parmesan cheese.

Spicy Pasta

Chicken Balls in Tomato Sauce

Preparation time:
  30 minutes
Cooking time:
  45 minutes
Serves 6

1 *pound ground*
  chicken
1 *onion, finely chopped*
1 *egg, beaten*
3 *tablespoons fine dry*
  bread crumbs
1/4 *teaspoon each dried*
  oregano and thyme,
  crushed
3 *tablespoons cooking*
  oil

Sauce
1 *tablespoon cooking*
  oil
1 *onion, chopped*
2 *tomatoes, peeled and*
  chopped
1 *cup tomato purée*
1 *cup water*
1 *tablespoon red wine*
  vinegar
1 *teaspoon instant*
  chicken bouillon
  granules
1 *teaspoon brown sugar*
1/2 *teaspoon chili powder*
Pinch *pepper*
1 *tablespoon cold water*
2 *teaspoons cornstarch*
1 *pound elbow*
  macaroni

1 In a bowl combine ground chicken, onion, egg, bread crumbs, oregano, and thyme. Mix till well combined.

Form chicken mixture into balls.
2 In a large skillet heat 3 tablespoons oil. Add meatballs, a few at a time, and cook till brown on all sides. Remove from skillet; drain on paper towels. Wipe skillet clean.
3 For sauce, heat 1 tablespoon oil in same skillet. Cook onion in oil till tender. Stir in tomatoes, tomato purée, water, vinegar, bouillon granules, brown sugar, chili powder, and pepper. Bring to a boil; reduce heat. Add meatballs to skillet and simmer for 5 minutes.
4 Meanwhile, cook pasta according to package directions or for 10 minutes or till al dente. Drain. Spoon warm pasta onto serving plates. Top with sauce and meatballs.

Note: Instead of frying, meatballs can also be broiled or baked in the oven till done.

24

Chicken Balls in Tomato Sauce

— FABULOUS SEAFOOD PASTA —

Almost Instant Tagliatelle

Caviar, anchovies, and fresh and canned fish and seafood can all be combined with many other flavors to produce exotic and delicious sauces suitable to serve over a bowl of steaming hot pasta.

A sprinkling of fresh herbs and freshly ground pepper is often the best topping since Parmesan cheese does not lend itself very well to fishy pasta dishes.

For best results, do not overcook fish or seafood or it will become tough and dry. It should be cooked just till tender and then served immediately.

Almost Instant Tagliatelle

Preparation time:
  5 minutes
Cooking time:
  8 minutes
Serves 4

12 ounces green
  tagliatelle pasta
6¹/4-ounce can water-
  pack tuna, drained
  and flaked
¹/3 cup melted butter or
  margarine
¹/4 cup chopped fresh
  parsley
1 tablespoon chopped
  fresh mixed herbs

2 cloves garlic,
  crushed
Freshly ground
  pepper

1 Cook pasta according to package directions or for 6 to 8 minutes or till al dente. Drain.
2 Add tuna, butter or margarine, parsley, herbs, garlic, and pepper, tossing to combine with pasta. Serve immediately.

Tagliatelle with Caviar

Preparation time:
  10 minutes
Cooking time:
  8 minutes
Serves 6

1 pound green or white
  tagliatelle pasta
¹/3 cup butter or
  margarine
Freshly ground
  pepper
8-ounce carton sour
  cream
1¹/2 ounces black caviar
1¹/2 ounces red caviar

1 Cook pasta according to package directions or for 6 to 8 minutes or till al dente. Drain. Add butter or margarine and pepper, tossing to combine.
2 To serve, arrange pasta on serving plates. Top with sour cream and caviar.

Tagliatelle with Caviar

Pasta with Mussels

Preparation time:
  25 minutes
Cooking time:
  30 minutes
Serves 4

Sauce
2 pounds fresh mussels
  in shells
1 large onion, chopped

1 cup dry red wine
2 tablespoons
  olive oil
2 tablespoons butter or
  margarine
4 ounces mushrooms,
  sliced
3 cloves garlic, crushed
2 x 14½-ounce cans
  chopped tomatoes
1 tablespoon tomato
  paste
2 tablespoons chopped
  fresh basil

2 tablespoons chopped
  fresh parsley
1 bay leaf
Freshly ground pepper
12 ounces farfalle (bow
  tie pasta)
¼ cup sour cream
  (optional)
Fresh lemon juice

1 Debeard mussels and
scrub shells with a stiff
brush under cold water
to remove grit. Discard

1 To debeard mussels, pull off the
hairy beards with your fingers.

2 Simmer mussels, onion, and wine
for 5 minutes or till mussels open.

3 Add tomato mixture and simmer
till thickened.

4 Combine cooked pasta and mussels
with sauce. Add sour cream, if desired.

any mussels that have open shells or shells that do not close when sharply tapped.

2 For sauce, in a saucepan combine mussels, half of the onion, and wine. Bring to a boil; reduce heat. Cover and simmer for 5 minutes or till mussels open. Strain, reserving liquid. Discard any unopened shells. Set mussels and liquid aside.

3 In a large skillet heat oil and butter or margarine over medium heat. Add remaining onion with mushrooms and garlic. Cover and cook till onion is tender. Add reserved mussel liquid, undrained tomatoes, tomato paste, basil, parsley, bay leaf, and pepper. Simmer, uncovered, till thickened, stirring occasionally. Discard bay leaf.

4 Cook pasta according to package directions or for 10 minutes or till al dente. Drain. Add sauce and reserved mussels to saucepan with pasta, tossing gently to combine. If desired, stir in sour cream. Add fresh lemon juice to taste. Garnish with fresh basil leaves.

Sicilian Spaghetti

Preparation time:
    10 minutes
Cooking time:
    15 minutes
Serves 4

5 *Serve Pasta with Mussels piping hot.*

Sicilian Spaghetti (left) and Pasta Marinara

1 pound spaghetti

Sauce
2-ounce can anchovy
  fillets
2 tablespoons
  olive oil
2 cloves garlic, crushed
2 tablespoons fine dry
  bread crumbs
Freshly ground
  pepper
Chopped fresh parsley
Grated Parmesan
  cheese

1 Cook pasta according to package directions or for 10 to 12 minutes or till al dente. Drain. Place in a warm serving dish.
2 For sauce, drain and chop anchovy fillets. In a saucepan heat oil. Cook garlic in oil till tender. Add anchovies and cook for 2 minutes. Stir in bread crumbs and pepper; heat through.
3 Spoon sauce over spaghetti and toss lightly. Sprinkle with chopped parsley and serve with Parmesan cheese.

Pasta Marinara

Preparation time:
  15 minutes
Cooking time:
  35 minutes
Serves 4

Sauce
1 tablespoon cooking
  oil
1 onion, finely
  chopped
2 cloves garlic,
  crushed
15-ounce can tomato
  purée
1 cup dry red wine
1 small carrot, coarsely
  shredded
1 stalk celery,
  chopped
1/2 teaspoon dried basil,
  crushed
Freshly ground pepper

12 ounces spaghetti
1¹/2 cups mixed
  uncooked seafood
  (shrimp, scallops,
  crabmeat, or mussels)

1 For sauce, in a saucepan heat oil. Add onions and cook till tender. Add garlic and cook for 1 minute. Stir in tomato purée, wine, carrot, celery, basil, and pepper. Bring to a boil; reduce heat. Simmer, uncovered, for 15 minutes.
2 Meanwhile, cook pasta according to package directions or for 10 to 12 minutes or till al dente. Drain. Place in a warm serving dish.
3 To assemble, add seafood to sauce. Cover and simmer for 2 to 5 minutes or till seafood is tender or mussels are open. Pour sauce over spaghetti and toss lightly.

Note: Pasta Marinara is not usually served with Parmesan cheese. However, if desired, you can stir a tablespoon or two of finely chopped parsley into the sauce.

Vermicelli Royale

Preparation time:
  10 minutes
Cooking time:
  12 minutes
Serves 2

8 ounces vermicelli

Sauce
1 cup heavy cream
2 tablespoons chopped
  shallots or green
  onions
Pinch paprika
Freshly ground pepper
2 ounces smoked
  salmon, cut into thin
  strips
2 teaspoons salmon or
  red lumpfish caviar
Fresh herbs

1 Cook pasta according to package directions or for 5 to 7 minutes or till al dente. Drain. Keep warm.
2 For sauce, in a small saucepan combine cream and shallots or onions. Bring to a boil; reduce heat. Simmer, uncovered, for 5 minutes. Stir in paprika and pepper.
3 Arrange pasta on warm serving plates. Stir salmon into cream mixture and spoon over pasta. Garnish with caviar and herbs.

Note: If you prefer, a tablespoon of finely chopped chives can be stirred into the sauce before adding salmon.

Vermicelli Royale

Macaroni Pizza

Macaroni Pizza

Preparation time:
  20 minutes
Soaking time:
  30 minutes
Cooking time:
  50 minutes
Serves 6

8 ounces elbow
  macaroni
2 x 2-ounce cans
  anchovy fillets

Sauce
2 tablespoons cooking
  oil
1 onion, finely
  chopped
1 clove garlic, chopped
14¹/2-ounce can
  chopped tomatoes
1 tablespoon tomato
  paste
¹/2 teaspoon dried basil,
  crushed
6 ounces sliced Swiss
  cheese
Sliced cherry tomatoes
Fresh basil

1 Cook pasta according
to package directions
or for 10 minutes or till
al dente. Drain. Keep
warm.
2 Drain anchovies.
Soak in a bowl of milk
for 30 minutes;
drain.
3 For sauce, in a
saucepan heat oil. Add
onion and garlic and
cook till tender. Add
undrained tomatoes,
tomato paste, and basil.
Cover and simmer for
20 minutes, stirring
occasionally. Remove
from heat.
4 Grease a 10-inch
round baking dish.
Spread half of the
cooked pasta in bottom
of dish. Spoon sauce
over pasta and top with
remaining pasta. Place
cheese slices over pasta
and arrange anchovies
in a lattice pattern over
the top. Put a cherry
tomato slice in each
square.
5 Bake, uncovered, in
a 375° oven for 15 to
20 minutes or till
heated through and
cheese melts. Let stand
5 minutes before
serving. Garnish with
fresh basil.

Bali-Style Noodles

Preparation time:
  20 minutes
Cooking time:
  20 minutes
Serves 6

1 pound capellini
  (angel hair
  pasta)
3 tablespoons cooking
  oil
1 large onion, *thinly
  sliced*
2 stalks celery, *thinly
  sliced*
1 green bell pepper,
  thinly sliced
1 red bell pepper, *thinly
  sliced*
1 to 2 fresh hot chilies,
  thinly sliced
3 tablespoons soy
  sauce
3 tablespoons dry
  sherry
1 pound cooked
  prawns *or large
  shrimp, peeled and
  deveined with tails
  intact*

1 Cook pasta according to package directions or for 4 to 5 minutes or till al dente. Drain. Keep warm.
2 In a large skillet heat oil. Cook sliced onion, celery, green pepper, red pepper, and hot chilies in oil till onion is tender. Add soy sauce and dry sherry. Add hot noodles and toss till well combined. Add prawns or shrimp and heat through.

Note: Different types of chili vary considerably in strength, so if you don't want a really hot dish, remove the seeds and ribs before slicing. Be sure to wash the knife and cutting board thoroughly after handling chilies.

Bali-Style Noodles

— PASTA WITH CREAM AND CHEESE —

Fabulous pasta served with butter and cheese

The delicate flavors of fresh cheese, cream, and milk combine deliciously with the stronger flavors of hard cheeses to form pasta sauces that can be made quickly.
Enrich sauces with a little egg yolk or bit of butter and a few seasonings and you will produce a memorable meal.

Buttered Noodles

Preparation time:
  5 minutes
Cooking time:
  12 minutes
Serves 6

1 pound fettuccine
1/4 cup butter or
  margarine
1 cup heavy cream
1 cup grated Parmesan
  cheese
Freshly ground pepper

1 Cook pasta according to package directions or for 8 to 10 minutes or till al dente. Drain. Keep warm.
2 In a small saucepan melt butter or margarine. Stir in cream, Parmesan cheese, and pepper. Cook and stir till heated through. Pour cream mixture over pasta, tossing to coat. Serve at once.

Noodle Bake

Preparation time:
  10 minutes
Cooking time:
  35 minutes
Serves 6

2 1/2 cups cooked egg
  noodles
1 cup cottage cheese
1 cup sour cream
1/2 cup sliced shallots
2 cups Rich Meat Sauce
  (see recipe) or
  purchased spaghetti
  sauce with meat
1 cup shredded cheddar
  cheese
Snipped fresh chives

1 In a bowl combine noodles, cottage cheese, sour cream, and shallots. Spoon into a greased shallow baking dish.
2 Pour meat sauce over noodle mixture. Sprinkle with cheese and chives. Bake, uncovered, in a 350° oven about 35 minutes or till heated through and bubbly.

HINT
Fresh cream can be soured by adding 1 teaspoon of vinegar per cup of cream.

Noodle Bake

Clockwise from left: Spaghetti Creole, Blue Cheese Tagliatelle, and Spaghetti Carbonara

Spaghetti Creole

Preparation time:
  15 minutes
Cooking time:
  30 minutes
Serves 4

Sauce
1/4 cup butter

1 pound prawns or
  large shrimp, in shells
14 1/2-ounce can
  chopped tomatoes
3 tablespoons grated
  Parmesan cheese
2 teaspoons curry
  powder
Freshly ground
  pepper
1 1/2 cups heavy
  cream

1 pound spaghetti

1 For sauce, in a skillet
melt butter. Cook
prawns or shrimp in
butter till just pink.
Remove from skillet
and set aside. Add
undrained tomatoes,
Parmesan cheese, curry
powder, and pepper.
Simmer for 10 minutes.

Return prawns or shrimp to sauce. Stir in cream; heat through.
2 Cook pasta according to package directions or for 10 to 12 minutes or till al dente. Drain. Return to pan. Add sauce, tossing over low heat for 1 to 2 minutes. Garnish with fresh parsley.

HINT
Devein shelled prawns or shrimp by cutting along the back with a sharp knife and removing the vein.

Spaghetti Carbonara

Preparation time:
  10 minutes
Cooking time:
  15 minutes
Serves 6

Sauce
8 slices bacon
1¹/4 cups heavy cream
4 egg yolks
3 tablespoons grated Parmesan cheese

1 pound spaghetti
Chopped fresh chives

1 For sauce, in a skillet cook bacon till crisp. Drain on paper towels. Drain fat from skillet.

Add cream to skillet. Bring to a boil; reduce heat. Simmer, uncovered, for 2 minutes. Remove from heat and stir in egg yolks and cheese. Crumble bacon into sauce; set aside.
2 Cook pasta according to package directions or for 10 to 12 minutes or till al dente. Drain. Return to pan. Add sauce, tossing over low heat for 1 to 2 minutes. Garnish with fresh chives.

Blue Cheese Tagliatelle

Preparation time:
  10 minutes
Cooking time:
  20 minutes
Serves 6

Sauce
2 tablespoons butter or margarine
2 zucchini, sliced
1 clove garlic, crushed
1¹/4 cups heavy cream
3¹/2 ounces blue cheese, crumbled
Freshly ground pepper
1/2 cup dry white wine

1 pound green or white tagliatelle
Chopped fresh parsley
Grated Parmesan cheese
1 For sauce, in a skillet melt butter or

---

margarine. Add zucchini and garlic and cook till zucchini is tender. Stir in cream, blue cheese, and pepper. Simmer for 10 minutes. Stir in wine and heat through (do not boil).
2 Cook pasta according to package directions or for 6 to 8 minutes or till al dente. Drain. Return to pan. Add sauce, tossing over low heat for 1 to 2 minutes. Garnish with fresh parsley and serve with Parmesan cheese.

Pasta, Eggs, and Mushrooms

Preparation time:
  20 minutes
Cooking time:
  35 minutes
Serves 4

12 ounces elbow macaroni
1 onion, sliced

Sauce
2 tablespoons butter or margarine
2 tablespoons all-purpose flour
1¹/2 cups milk
1/8 teaspoon ground red pepper
1/4 cup shredded cheddar cheese
4 ounces small mushrooms, sliced
1 tablespoon butter or margarine

Pasta, Eggs, and Mushrooms

4 hard-cooked eggs
1 cup soft bread crumbs
¹/4 cup melted butter or
  margarine

1 Cook pasta according to package directions except add onion to boiling water with macaroni and cook for 10 minutes or till al dente. Drain.
2 Meanwhile, for sauce, in a saucepan melt 2 tablespoons butter or margarine. Stir in flour. Add milk and red pepper all at once. Cook and stir till thickened and bubbly. Cook and stir 1 minute more. Stir in cheese till melted.
3 In a small saucepan cook mushrooms in 1 tablespoon butter or margarine till tender. Add mushrooms and pasta mixture to sauce.
4 To assemble, spoon half of the pasta mixture into a greased shallow baking dish. Halve eggs lengthwise and arrange over pasta, cut side down. Cover with remaining pasta mixture.
5 Toss bread crumbs with ¹/4 cup melted butter or margarine. Sprinkle over top of pasta. Bake, uncovered, in a 375° oven for 15 minutes or till bread crumbs are golden brown and pasta mixture is heated through.

HINT
For a less spicy dish, ¹/2 teaspoon chili powder can be substituted for the ground red pepper.

Spinach Gnocchi

Preparation time:
  40 minutes
Cooking time:
  45 minutes
Serves 4

1¹/2 *pounds fresh
  spinach, cleaned,
  trimmed and finely
  chopped*
*15-ounce carton ricotta
  cheese*
2 eggs
*1 cup grated Parmesan
  cheese*
Freshly ground pepper
Pinch ground nutmeg
All-purpose flour
1/4 cup butter, melted

1 In a bowl combine
spinach, ricotta cheese,
eggs, half of the
Parmesan cheese,
pepper, and nutmeg.
Mix till well combined.
2 On a lightly floured
surface and with
floured hands, shape
spinach mixture into
2-inch balls. Lightly
coat balls with flour to
prevent sticking. Set
aside on waxed paper.
3 Bring a large
saucepan of water to a
boil; reduce heat. Drop
3 or 4 gnocchi into
simmering water.
Simmer until they float
to the surface. Remove
with a slotted spoon
and drain briefly and
transfer to a greased
shallow baking dish.

Spinach Gnocchi

Repeat with remaining
gnocchi.
4 Top gnocchi in baking
dish with remaining
Parmesan cheese and
drizzle with butter.
Bake, uncovered, in a
400° oven 15 minutes.

> ### HINT
> Fresh herbs give
> sauces an
> exceptional flavor,
> so when possible,
> use fresh herbs
> instead of dried. Use
> three times as much
> fresh as dried. For
> instance 1 teaspoon
> dried herb equals
> 3 teaspoons (or
> 1 tablespoon) fresh
> herb.

Noodle Shell Quiche

Preparation time:
  25 minutes
Cooking time:
  45 minutes
Serves 4

*12 ounces spaghettini
  (very thin spaghetti),
  broken into
  pieces*
*8 ounces bacon, cut
  into 2-inch pieces*
1 onion, chopped
4 eggs
1³/4 cups milk
*1 cup shredded Swiss
  cheese*
*1/2 cup grated Parmesan
  cheese*

Noodle Shell Quiche (left) and Pasta with Broccoli (right)

¹/₂ teaspoon dried basil, crushed
¹/₄ teaspoon pepper
Pinch ground nutmeg

1 Cook pasta according to package directions or for 8 to 10 minutes or till al dente. Drain. Place pasta in a buttered 10-inch quiche dish or shallow baking dish.
2 In a skillet cook bacon till crisp; drain on paper towels. Drain bacon drippings, reserving 1 tablespoon in skillet. Cook onion in bacon drippings till tender. Sprinkle bacon and onion over pasta in dish.
3 In a bowl whisk together eggs and milk. Stir in Swiss cheese, Parmesan cheese, basil, pepper, and nutmeg. Slowly pour over pasta mixture in dish.
4 Bake, uncovered, in a 350° oven for 30 minutes or till a knife inserted near the center comes out clean. Let stand 10 minutes before serving.

Pasta with Broccoli

Preparation time:
  15 minutes
Cooking time:
  20 minutes
Serves 6

Sauce
3 tablespoons butter or margarine
1 tablespoon all-purpose flour
¹/₄ teaspoon dried basil, crushed
¹/₄ teaspoon dried oregano, crushed

*Freshly ground
  pepper*
1 1/2 *cups milk*
8 *ounces ricotta
  cheese*
4 *ounces mozzarella
  cheese, diced*

1 *pound fettuccine*
3 *cups broccoli
  flowerets*
1/4 *cup sliced shallots*
8 *ounces cherry
  tomatoes, halved
  (optional)*
3 *tablespoons chopped
  fresh parsley*

1 For sauce, in a saucepan melt butter or margarine. Add flour, basil, oregano, and pepper. Stir in milk. Cook and stir till thickened and bubbly. Cook and stir 1 minute more. Add cheeses and cook over low heat till melted and well combined.
2 Cook pasta according to package directions or for 8 to 10 minutes or till al dente. Add broccoli to pasta water during the last 5 minutes of cooking. Drain pasta and broccoli. Toss pasta and broccoli with shallots and if desired, tomatoes. Spoon into a serving dish. Pour sauce over pasta mixture. Garnish with parsley. (If sauce becomes too thick, thin with milk, 1 tablespoon at a time.)

Parsley Garlic Noodles

Preparation time:
  20 minutes
Cooking time:
  8 minutes
Serves 6

Sauce
1/3 *cup dry white wine*
3 *slices thick white
  bread, crusts removed
  and torn into pieces*
1 *cup chopped fresh
  parsley*
3 *cloves garlic, crushed*
1/4 *teaspoon pepper*
1/2 *cup olive oil*

1 *pound fettuccine*

1 For sauce, sprinkle wine over bread and let stand for 10 minutes. Cut soaked bread into pieces.
2 In a bowl combine parsley, garlic, and pepper. Gradually add olive oil, stirring till well combined. Add bread mixture, a little at a time, beating with an electric mixer after each addition till smooth and thick. Set aside.
3 Cook pasta according to package directions or for 8 to 10 minutes or till al dente. Drain. Transfer to a warm serving bowl. Spoon sauce over pasta, tossing to combine.

HINT
Pasta should always be cooked in rapidly boiling water. However, when cooking gnocchi, make sure the water is only simmering because rapidly boiling water will break it up.

Parsley Garlic Noodles

— PASTA AND VEGETABLES —

Spaghetti Napoletana

Combine the versatility of pasta with the endless variety of vegetables and you have the basis of many delicious meals. The range of interesting combinations here will please vegetarians and non-vegetarians alike.

Spaghetti Napoletana

Preparation time:
   20 minutes
Cooking time:
   20 minutes
Serves 4

1 pound spaghetti

Sauce
2 tablespoons cooking oil
1 onion, sliced
2 cloves garlic, crushed
1 pound tomatoes, peeled and coarsely chopped
1 teaspoon sugar
1 bay leaf
Freshly ground pepper
1 teaspoon chopped fresh basil
Parmesan cheese
Fresh parsley

1 Cook pasta according to package directions or for 10 to 12 minutes or till al dente. Drain. Keep warm.
2 Meanwhile, for sauce, in a saucepan heat oil. Cook onion and garlic in oil till tender. Add tomatoes, sugar, bay leaf, and pepper. Cover and simmer till tomatoes are soft. Stir in basil and remove bay leaf.
3 Transfer cooked pasta to a warm serving bowl. Pour sauce over pasta and toss lightly. Serve with Parmesan cheese and garnish with fresh parsley.

Spaghetti with Spinach Sauce

Preparation time:
   15 minutes
Cooking time:
   20 minutes
Serves 4

1 pound spaghetti

Sauce
1 tablespoon cooking oil
3 cloves garlic, crushed
2 x 10-ounce packages frozen spinach, thawed and drained
1/2 cup grated Parmesan cheese
2 teaspoons dried basil, crushed
3 ounces pine nuts

1 Cook pasta according to package directions or for 10 to 12 minutes or till al dente. Drain. Keep warm.
2 For sauce, in a large skillet heat oil. Cook garlic in oil till tender. Add spinach, cheese, and basil. Cook about 5 minutes or till heated through.
3 Transfer cooked pasta to a warm serving bowl. Spoon sauce over pasta. Sprinkle with pine nuts.

Spaghetti with Spinach Sauce

Ricotta Lasagna Swirls

Preparation time:
   45 minutes
Cooking time:
   40 minutes
Serves 6

12 lasagna noodles
1 pound fresh spinach,
   washed and chopped
   or 10-ounce package
   frozen chopped
   spinach, thawed and
   well drained
1 1/2 cups ricotta
   cheese
2 cups shredded
   mozzarella cheese
1 large egg, lightly
   beaten
2 tablespoons grated
   Parmesan cheese
1/4 teaspoon ground
   nutmeg
1/4 teaspoon pepper
1/4 cup butter or
   margarine
8 ounces small
   mushrooms,
   quartered
16-ounce jar meatless
   spaghetti sauce
1/2 cup dry red wine,
   beef broth, or chicken
   broth
1/2 teaspoon dried
   oregano, crushed
1/2 teaspoon dried basil,
   crushed

1 Cook pasta according to package directions or for 10 to 12 minutes or till al dente. Drain and rinse with cold water.

Ricotta Lasagna Swirls (left) and Pasta Caprese

Place noodles in a bowl of cold water.
2 In a large saucepan steam fresh spinach over simmering water for 5 to 7 minutes or till cooked. Drain well, pressing out liquid. In a bowl combine drained spinach, ricotta cheese, half of the mozzarella cheese, egg, Parmesan cheese, nutmeg, and pepper. Set aside.
3 In a skillet melt butter or margarine. Cook mushrooms in skillet till

just tender. Remove from heat and cool. Drain. Stir together spaghetti sauce, wine or broth, oregano, and basil. Spoon half of the mixture into a 13 x 9 x 2-inch baking dish. Remove 1 noodle at a time from water and drain on paper towels. Spread each noodle with about 2 rounded tablespoons of the ricotta mixture. Place a spoonful of mushrooms along one of the short

44

1 red bell pepper, thinly
  sliced
3 cloves garlic,
  crushed
1 tablespoon chopped
  fresh basil
1/2 cup olive oil
Freshly ground
  pepper

1 pound rotelle
  (corkscrew
  pasta)
4 ounces mozzarella
  cheese, cut into small
  squares
Grated Parmesan
  cheese

1 For sauce, in a bowl
combine tomatoes,
bell pepper, garlic, and
basil. Add oil and
pepper, stirring till
well combined. Cover
and let stand at room
temperature for
1 hour.
2 Cook pasta
according to package
directions or for 8 to
10 minutes or till al
dente. Drain. Add
mozzarella cheese to
hot pasta. Place in a
serving dish; top with
sauce. Serve with
Parmesan cheese.

sides and roll up noodle
around cheese and
mushroom mixture.
Place, seam side down,
in baking dish. Spoon
remaining sauce over
lasagna rolls.
4 Cover and bake in a
350° oven for 20
minutes. Remove foil or
lid and sprinkle with
remaining mozzarella
cheese and top with any
remaining mushrooms.
Bake, uncovered, for
5 to 10 minutes more or
till cheese melts.

Pasta Caprese

Preparation time:
  15 minutes
Standing time:
  1 hour
Cooking time:
  10 minutes
Serves 6

Sauce
12 roma tomatoes or
  4 large tomatoes,
  thinly sliced

Pasta Tomato Bocconcini (left) and Spirals with Potatoes and Spinach

Pasta Tomato Bocconcini

Preparation time:
  10 minutes
Cooking time:
  10 minutes
Serves 4

12 ounces rigatoni
1 tablespoon olive oil

Tomato Bocconcini
4 ripe tomatoes, peeled,
  seeded, cut into chunks
1 pound fresh
  mozzarella cheese
  (bocconcini), cut into
  small cubes

12 pitted ripe olives
1/4 teaspoon dried
  oregano, crushed
1/4 teaspoon dried basil,
  crushed
Freshly ground pepper
2 tablespoons olive oil

1 Cook pasta according
to package directions or

for 15 minutes or till al dente. Drain. Return to pan and stir in 1 tablespoon olive oil. Cool.

2 To prepare bocconcini, in a bowl combine tomatoes, mozzarella, olives, oregano, basil, and pepper. Drizzle with 2 tablespoons olive oil and toss gently to combine.

3 Toss mozzarella mixture with cooled pasta and place in a serving bowl.

> ### HINT
> Extra virgin olive oil is the best to use as a flavoring oil in pasta dishes, such as Pasta Tomato Bocconcini. For cooking, it is better to use less expensive pure olive oil.

Spirals with Potatoes and Spinach

Preparation time:
  20 minutes
Cooking time:
  15 minutes
Serves 4

12 ounces rotelle
  (corkscrew pasta)
8 ounces new potatoes,
  peeled and thickly
  sliced

> ### HINT
> Purchase corn wrapped in its husks because the husk will keep the corn fresher longer. Avoid purchasing corn wrapped in plastic wrap since it makes the corn sweat, causing it to lose moisture and dry out when cooked.

2 tablespoons olive oil
1 clove garlic, crushed
2 dried red chilies,
  finely chopped
1/2 bunch fresh spinach,
  trimmed, washed, and
  coarsely chopped
Freshly ground pepper

1 In a large saucepan or Dutch oven cook pasta and potato slices in boiling water for 10 minutes or till pasta is al dente and potatoes are tender. Drain. Place in a warm serving bowl.

2 In a saucepan heat oil. Add garlic and chilies and cook for 1 to 2 minutes. Add spinach and cook and stir over high heat for 1 minute or till wilted. Add to pasta mixture in bowl, tossing to combine. Season with pepper.

Mexican Pasta

Preparation time:
  15 minutes
Cooking time:
  20 minutes
Serves 6

2 tablespoons butter or
  margarine
1 onion, thinly
  sliced
1 red bell pepper,
  thickly sliced
3 stalks celery, cut
  into 3/4-inch pieces
2 fresh ears corn, cut
  into 3/4-inch slices
1 pound conchiglie
  (medium shell
  pasta)
2 cups water
1 1/4-ounce envelope
  taco seasoning mix

1 In a saucepan melt butter or margarine. Add onion, bell pepper, and celery and cook till onion is tender.

2 Add corn, uncooked pasta, water, and taco seasoning mix. Bring to a boil and cook for 15 minutes or till pasta is al dente and corn is tender.

> ### HINT
> Leave the skin on potatoes for added color, fiber, and flavor.

− *FRESH PASTA SALADS* −

Mediterranean Salad (left) and Macaroni Salad (right)

*P*asta is delicious in salads. Combined with meats such as chicken or ham or with crunchy vegetables, pasta's tender yet firm texture adds variety. The following recipes are perfect for summer nights on the patio or a barbecue cook out.

Macaroni Salad

Preparation time:
  15 minutes
Cooking time:
  14 minutes
Serves 4

12 ounces conchiglie
  (medium shell pasta)
1/2 to 1 cup bottled
  Italian salad dressing
15-ounce can three-
  bean salad, rinsed and
  drained
1/2 cup pimiento-stuffed
  green olives, sliced
4 stalks celery, sliced
1 small white onion,
  finely chopped
2 tablespoons chopped
  fresh parsley

1 Cook pasta according to package directions or for 12 to 14 minutes or till al dente. Drain in a colander and rinse with cold water; drain. Transfer to a large bowl. Stir in enough Italian salad dressing to moisten.
2 Drain bean salad in a colander and rinse under water. Drain. Add to pasta mixture with olives, celery, and onion. Drizzle on a little more salad dressing, tossing to coat. Cover and chill till serving time.
3 Before serving, sprinkle with chopped fresh parsley.

Mediterranean Salad

Preparation time:
  20 minutes
Cooking time:
  10 minutes
Serves 6

1 pound penne pasta
2 tablespoons olive oil
1 small red bell pepper,
  cut into thin strips
3 ounces pepperoni, cut
  into thin strips
1 tomato, coarsely
  chopped
1 cup shredded zucchini
1 cup shredded
  provolone or cheddar
  cheese
1/2 cup chopped fresh
  parsley
8 pitted ripe olives,
  sliced

1/4 cup finely chopped
  onion

Vinaigrette
1/3 cup olive oil
3 tablespoons red wine
  vinegar
1 clove garlic, crushed
2 tablespoons chopped
  fresh basil or 2
  teaspoons dried basil,
  crushed
1 teaspoon chopped
  fresh oregano or
  1/4 teaspoon dried
  oregano, crushed
Freshly ground pepper

1 Cook pasta according to package directions or for 15 minutes or till al dente. Drain in a colander and rinse with cold water; drain. Transfer to a large bowl. Stir in 2 tablespoons olive oil.
2 Stir in bell pepper, pepperoni, tomato, zucchini, cheese, parsley, olives and onion.
3 For vinaigrette, in a bowl whisk together

HINT
Bell peppers are delicious roasted. Halve peppers and remove seeds and membranes. Place under the broiler, skin side up, till skin turns black. Place in a clean paper bag and seal. When cool, remove and discard the skin.

oil, vinegar, garlic, basil, and oregano till well combined. Pour over pasta mixture and toss till well combined. Season with pepper. Cover and chill till serving time.

Ham and Pasta Salad

Preparation time:
  15 minutes
Chilling time:
  Overnight
Cooking time:
  15 minutes
Serves 6

Dressing
3/4 cup olive oil
3 tablespoons red wine vinegar
2 tablespoons lemon juice
2 tablespoons chopped fresh basil or 1 teaspoon dried basil
1/2 teaspoon pepper

1 pound penne pasta
3 medium carrots, cut into julienne strips
2 medium zucchini, cut into julienne strips
6 ounces cooked sliced ham, cut into short strips

1 For dressing, in a screw-top jar combine oil, vinegar, lemon juice, basil, and pepper. Cover and shake till well combined.

2 Cook pasta according to package directions or for 15 minutes or till al dente. Drain in a colander and rinse with cold water; drain. Transfer to a bowl.
3 Pour dressing over warm pasta, tossing to coat. Cover and chill overnight, stirring occasionally.
4 Before serving, cook carrots and zucchini in boiling water for 2 minutes. Drain and rinse under cold water. Drain well. Add to pasta mixture with ham and stir till well combined.

Chicken Pasta Bowl

Preparation time:
  20 minutes
Cooking time:
  10 minutes
Serves 6

1 pound macaroni
3 cups steamed vegetables
2 cups diced cooked chicken
6 ounces cheddar cheese, cubed
2 stalks celery, sliced

Dressing
1/2 cup salad oil
1/4 cup tarragon vinegar
2 tablespoons chopped shallots
2 tablespoons chopped fresh parsley

1/2 teaspoon sugar
1/2 teaspoon dried marjoram, crushed
1/4 teaspoon dried mustard
1/4 teaspoon pepper

1 Cook pasta according to package directions or for 10 minutes or till al dente. Drain in a colander and rinse with cold water; drain. Cool; transfer to serving bowl.
2 Add vegetables, chicken, cheese, and celery to pasta.
3 For dressing, in a screw-top jar combine oil, vinegar, shallots, parsley, sugar, marjoram, mustard, and pepper. Cover and shake till well combined. Pour over pasta mixture, tossing to coat. Chill several hours before serving.

Garden Pasta Salad with Frankfurters

Preparation time:
  15 minutes
Cooking time:
  15 minutes
Serves 4

12 ounces penne or ziti pasta
1 small bunch fresh asparagus, trimmed and cut into 1 1/2-inch pieces
3 frankfurters or hot dogs, sliced

2 cups cooked
   vegetables (carrots,
   green beans, peas, or
   corn)
Mayonnaise
Freshly ground pepper

1 Cook pasta according
to package directions
or for 15 minutes or till al dente. Drain; rinse
with cold water; drain.
2 In a large saucepan
cook asparagus and
frankfurters in
simmering water till
asparagus is crisp-
tender. Drain well.
3 In a large bowl
combine cooked pasta, asparagus-frankfurter
mixture, and mixed
vegetables. Add enough
mayonnaise to moisten
salad, tossing to coat.
Season with pepper.
Serve immediately or
cover and chill till
serving time.

Chicken Pasta Bowl (left) and Ham and Pasta Salad (right)

— DESSERT PASTAS —

Flambéed Bows in Orange Liqueur Cream Sauce

*T*raditionally, pasta is considered a food served as a savory dish but this needn't always be the case. Here is a selection of sweet pastas that are boiled, baked, or fried to tempt the fussiest taste buds.

Whenever possible, do not serve a pasta dessert after a pasta meal. Pasta desserts make a grand finale to a light and simple meal.

Flambéed Bows in Orange Liqueur Cream Sauce

Preparation time:
  15 minutes
Cooking time:
  10 minutes
Serves 8

1 pound fresh or refrigerated farfalle (bow tie pasta) or 8 ounces dried pasta
1 orange
1 lemon
1/2 cup butter
1/2 cup sugar
2 tablespoons all-purpose flour
1 cup milk
3 tablespoons heavy cream
3 tablespoons Irish cream liqueur
3 tablespoons orange liqueur, warmed
Vanilla ice cream

1 Cook pasta according to package directions or for 2 to 3 minutes for fresh or 10 minutes for dried or till al dente. Drain and rinse with cold water; drain.
2 For sauce, finely shred peel of orange and lemon. Squeeze juice from orange and lemon and set aside.
3 In a large chafing dish melt butter. Stir in sugar, orange peel, and lemon peel. Cook over low heat for 2 to 3 minutes. Stir in flour. Add milk and cream. Cook and stir till thickened and bubbly. Cook and stir 1 minute more. Pour in Irish cream liqueur. Stir in drained pasta and citrus juices.
4 Add warm orange liqueur to pasta mixture. Ignite with a match. When flames subside, stir and serve warm with vanilla ice cream.

Spiced Orzo Pudding

Preparation time:
  15 minutes
Cooking time:
  50 minutes
Serves 6

4 ounces orzo (see Note)
1 1/2 cups milk
1 cup heavy cream
1/4 cup sugar
4-inch strip orange peel

1 cinnamon stick
1/2 teaspoon cardamom seed
2 tablespoons butter or margarine
3 eggs, separated
1/2 cup sugar
2 teaspoons orange flower water (optional)
Ice cream

1 In a saucepan combine orzo, milk, cream, sugar, orange peel, cinnamon stick, and cardamom seed. Bring to a boil; reduce heat. Simmer, uncovered, for 15 minutes or till orzo is tender. Remove from heat and stir in butter or margarine.
2 Grease a shallow 2-quart baking dish. When orzo mixture is cool, remove cinnamon stick and orange peel. Stir in beaten egg yolks. Pour into prepared dish. Bake, uncovered, in a 350° oven 15 minutes.
3 In a bowl beat egg whites with an electric mixer till soft peaks form. Gradually beat in 1/2 cup sugar, 1 tablespoon at a time, till stiff peaks form. If desired, beat in orange flower water.
4 Spoon egg white mixture over hot baked orzo mixture. Return to oven and bake for 5 to 10 minutes more or till egg white mixture is golden brown and set. Serve warm with ice cream.

Spiced Orzo Pudding (top) and Apple Cream Lasagna

Note: Orzo is a pasta that resembles rice in appearance. Look for it in the pasta aisle of your supermarket.

Apple Cream Lasagna

Preparation time:
  40 minutes
Cooking time:
  40 minutes
Serves 12

Apple Layer
21-ounce can apple pie filling
1/4 cup packed brown sugar
1 teaspoon ground cinnamon
1/3 cup coarsely chopped pecans

Cream Layer
8 ounces cream cheese

1/4 cup packed brown sugar
2 eggs
1 cup heavy cream
1 teaspoon vanilla

Crumb Topping
1/4 cup butter or margarine
8 slices whole wheat bread, crumbled
1/2 cup sugar
6 lasagna noodles, cooked, rinsed, and drained

1 For apple layer, in a bowl combine pie filling, 1/4 cup brown sugar, and cinnamon. Stir in pecans; set aside.

2 For cream layer, in a bowl beat softened cream cheese and 1/4 cup brown sugar with an electric mixer till fluffy. Add eggs, cream, and vanilla and beat on high speed 3 to 5 minutes or till thick; set aside.

3 For topping, in a large skillet melt butter or margarine. Add bread crumbs and cook for 2 to 3 minutes or till brown and crispy. Add sugar and cook 1 minute more. Cool.

4 To assemble, grease an 11 x 7 x 2-inch baking dish. Spoon half of the apple mixture in the bottom of prepared dish. Cover with 2 lasagna noodles. Spread half of the cream mixture over the lasagna and top with 2 more lasagna noodles. Sprinkle half of the crumbs over lasagna and top with remaining apple mixture. Top with 2 more lasagna noodles and remaining cream. Sprinkle with remaining crumbs.

5 Bake, uncovered, in a 350° oven for 35 to 40 minutes or till golden brown. Let stand 15 minutes before serving. Cut into squares and serve warm with vanilla ice cream.

Tropical Dip with Pasta Triangles

Preparation time:
  25 minutes
Cooking time:
  10 minutes
Serves 8

Dip
8-ounce container sour
  cream
8-ounce can crushed
  pineapple, drained
1 cup shredded coconut
Pulp of 2 passion fruit
  or 1 mango
6 ounces
  marshmallows,
  chopped
1 recipe fresh Almond
  Pasta (see page 9)
Oil for deep-fat frying
Sifted powdered sugar

1 For dip, in a bowl stir together sour cream, pineapple, coconut, passion fruit or mango, and marshmallows. Cover and chill for 1 hour before serving.

2 For pasta, prepare according to recipe directions. Roll out pasta with a rolling pin till thin or use a pasta machine and roll out to the second thinnest setting. Cut pasta into 3-inch squares. Cut each square in half diagonally to form a triangle.

3 Deep-fry pasta triangles, a few at a time, in hot oil (375°) till golden and crispy. Drain on paper towels. Sprinkle with powdered sugar. Serve with dip.

Tropical Dip with Pasta Triangles

Pasta Stuffed with Spicy Nut Filling

Preparation time:
  20 minutes
Chilling time:
  30 minutes
Cooking time:
  45 minutes
Makes 14 filled shells

14 *jumbo pasta shells*
(conchiglioni)
Crème a l'Anglaise (see
recipe following)

Filling
1¹/2 *cups cake crumbs*
4 *ounces walnuts or*
  pecans, ground
4 *ounces almonds,*
  ground
2 *tablespoons sugar*
¹/4 *teaspoon ground*
  cinnamon
¹/4 *teaspoon ground*
  nutmeg
¹/4 *teaspoon ground*
  ginger
Lightly beaten egg white
Oil for deep-fat frying

1 Cook pasta according to package directions or till al dente. Drain; rinse.
2 For filling, in a bowl combine cake crumbs, walnuts or pecans, almonds, sugar, cinnamon, nutmeg, and ginger. Moisten with egg white till mixture just holds together.
3 To assemble, spoon about 1 tablespoon filling into each pasta shell. Press 2 filled shells

Pasta Stuffed with Spicy Nut Filling

together. Arrange on a tray and chill, uncovered, for 30 minutes.
4 Deep-fry shells, a few at a time, in hot oil (375°) for 3 to 5 minutes or till golden brown. Drain on paper towels and serve with Crème a l'Anglaise.

Crème a l'Anglaise

Preparation time:
  10 minutes
Cooking time:
  10 minutes
Makes 1³/4 cups

¹/2 *cup heavy cream*
¹/2 *cup milk*
3 *egg yolks*
¹/4 *cup milk*
3 *tablespoons sugar*
1 *tablespoon cornstarch*
3 *tablespoons orange*
  liqueur

1 Combine cream and ¹/2 cup milk. Bring to a boil; remove from heat.
2 In another bowl combine egg yolks, ¹/4 cup milk, sugar, and cornstarch. Beat with an electric mixer or a wire whisk till well combined.

Pour a little hot cream mixture into egg yolk mixture, stirring constantly. Add all of egg yolk mixture to saucepan. 3 Cook and stir over medium heat till thickened and bubbly. Cook and stir 2 minutes more. Remove from heat and stir in orange liqueur. Serve immediately or cover surface with clear plastic wrap and chill till serving time.

Almond Tortellini with Fresh Fruit and Mascarpone

Preparation time:
  45 minutes
Cooking time:
  20 minutes
Serves 6

1 *pound fresh mascarpone (see Note)*
8 *ounces sour cream*
1 *cup honey*
8 *ounces strawberries, washed and hulled*
4 *kiwifruit, peeled and quartered*
1 *recipe fresh Almond Pasta (see page 9)*
1 *egg white*
1/4 *cup sugar*
2 *cups flaked coconut*
Oil for deep-fat frying

1 Beat together mascarpone and sour cream. Spoon mixture into 6 small serving dishes and drizzle 2 tablespoons of honey over tops. Arrange fruit on individual serving plates; cover and chill. 2 For pasta, prepare according to recipe directions. Roll out thinly and cut into 4-inch circles. Cover with a moist cloth and set aside. 3 In a bowl beat egg white till soft peaks form. Gradually add sugar and beat till stiff peaks form. Fold in coconut. Spoon about 1 tablespoon mixture on each circle of pasta dough. Brush edge of pasta with a little water. Fold pasta in half over filling, pressing edges together to seal. 4 Deep-fry pasta, a few at a time, in hot oil (375°) till golden brown. Drain on paper towels. Serve warm with fruit and mascarpone.

Note: Mascarpone is a rich cream product with a soft, creamy texture and slightly acidic flavor, similar to sour cream.

Almond Tortellini with Fresh Fruit and Mascarpone

— PERFECT ACCOMPANIMENTS —

Clockwise from top: a typical Antipasto Platter (all of the ingredients shown are available from delicatessens), Italian Bread and Italian-Style Salad.

This chapter contains recipes for entrées, accompaniments, and sweets, none of which contain pasta in their ingredients. They have been chosen because they are predominantly Italian and go so well with pasta.

The addition of one of these recipes to your pasta main course will help you compose a wonderful Italian meal.

The Antipasto Platter

Antipasto is the selection of hors d'oeuvres served at the beginning of the meal. The antipasto platter can be as simple or elaborate as you wish to make it.

Italian and supermarket delicatessens have a wide range of foods suitable for your next antipasto platter. These choices include:

Sliced salami
Olives
Anchovies
Ham
Marinated artichoke
 hearts
Marinated mushrooms
Pimientos
Antipasto vegetables
Thinly sliced cheese
Sun-dried tomatoes

Other additions to an antipasto platter could include figs or melons wrapped in thin slices of prosciutto or Parma ham, lightly fried eggplant pieces, cucumber chunks, cooked cubed potatoes, sliced onion, sliced fennel, radishes, and hard-cooked eggs.

Another popular antipasto ingredient is fresh seafood that is cooked and marinated in oil and vinegar or lightly coated with mayonnaise.

Arrange your antipasto platter to get an attractive contrast of colors, textures, and shapes.

Italian-Style Salad

Preparation time:
 10 minutes
Cooking time: None
Serves 8

Salad
1 head Romaine lettuce
1 head radicchio
1/4 bunch endive
1 fennel bulb, thinly
 sliced

8 ounces cherry
 tomatoes, washed
1 red onion, thinly
 sliced
1 red bell pepper, thinly
 sliced
1 small cucumber,
 thickly sliced

Italian Dressing
1/2 teaspoon finely
 shredded lemon peel
1/4 cup lemon juice
1/4 cup olive oil
1 clove garlic, crushed
1 tablespoon grated
 Parmesan cheese
1 teaspoon chopped
 fresh oregano
1/4 teaspoon pepper

1 Wash Romaine, radicchio, and endive thoroughly; pat dry with paper towels. Arrange leaves on a large serving platter. Arrange fennel, tomatoes, onion, bell pepper, and cucumber over leaves.
2 For dressing, in a screw-top jar combine lemon peel, lemon juice, oil, garlic, Parmesan cheese, oregano, and pepper. Cover and shake till well combined. Pour over salad.

> **HINT**
> Use any of the lovely salad greens in season to make this salad, including leaf lettuce, butter lettuce, sorrel, and spinach.

Fresh Pears Poached in White Wine (left) and Zabaglione (right).

Fresh Pears Poached in White Wine

Preparation time:
 15 minutes
Cooking time:
 20 minutes
Serves 4

4 *ripe pears*
2 *cups water*
1 *cup dry white wine*
1 *cup sugar*
1 *cinnamon stick*
1 *strip lemon peel*

1 Peel pears, leaving stems attached. Remove core of pears with an apple corer, leaving pears intact.
2 In a large saucepan combine water, wine, sugar, cinnamon stick, and lemon peel. Bring to a boil. Add pears; reduce heat. Simmer gently, uncovered, for 5 to 10 minutes or till firm but tender when tested with a skewer (cooking time depends on ripeness of pears). Remove pears with a slotted spoon. Set pears aside.
3 Bring pear liquid to a boil. Boil rapidly for 5 to 10 minutes or till slightly thickened. Spoon liquid over pears and serve warm or chilled

Zabaglione

Preparation time:
10 minutes
Cooking time:
5 minutes
Serves 4

6 egg yolks
1/4 cup sugar
3/4 cup marsala wine or
  cream sherry
Lady fingers or fresh
  fruit

1 In a heatproof bowl combine egg yolks and sugar. Whisk until pale yellow and well combined. Stir in marsala or cream sherry.
2 Place bowl over a pan of simmering water. Whisk constantly with a hand-held whisk or small electric mixer for 6 to 8 minutes or till thick and frothy and mixture starts to mound slightly. Pour immediately into individual stemmed glasses. Serve with lady fingers or fresh fruit.

HINT
Almond macaroons or small, crisp butter cookies also make a delicious accompaniment to this light, traditional Italian dessert.

Lemon Water Ice

Preparation time:
20 minutes plus
  freezing time
Cooking time:
5 minutes
Serves 6

2 1/2 cups water
3/4 cup sugar
1 1/4 cups freshly
  squeezed lemon juice

1 In a saucepan combine water and sugar. Bring to a boil. Boil rapidly for 5 minutes. Remove from heat and cool to room temperature. Stir in lemon juice. Cover and chill till needed.

2 Transfer mixture to a shallow metal tray; place in the coldest part of the freezer. Stir every 30 minutes until mixture is frozen firm. Transfer to an airtight container. Cover and store in the freezer till serving time.
3 To serve, scoop lemon ice into chilled glasses or a fresh lemon basket. Garnish with edible flowers.

HINT
Scoop flesh out of lemon halves after juicing and fill them with Lemon Water Ice. Cover and store in the freezer till serving time.

Lemon Water Ice

Italian Bread

Preparation time:
  10 minutes
Cooking time:
  15 minutes
Serves 12

16-ounce loaf French
  bread
2 tablespoons olive oil
1/3 cup butter or
  margarine, softened
2 anchovy fillets,
  drained and finely
  chopped
2 cloves garlic,
  crushed
2 tablespoons chopped
  fresh basil
2 tablespoons chopped
  fresh flat-leaf parsley
1/2 teaspoon pepper
1/4 cup grated Parmesan
  cheese

1 Halve bread horizontally. Place bread halves, cut side up, on a baking sheet. Drizzle or brush with oil.
2 In a bowl combine butter or margarine, anchovies, garlic, basil, parsley, and pepper. Spread butter mixture over cut side of each bread half. Sprinkle with Parmesan cheese.
3 Bake, uncovered, in a 400° oven for 15 minutes or till butter and cheese melt and brown lightly. Cut each half into 6 pieces and serve warm.

Italian Bread

Hint
Flat-leaf or Italian parsley has a strong, distinct flavor. The more common curly-leaf variety is an acceptable substitute.

Hint
When chopping fresh chilies, it is best to wear rubber gloves to protect your hands. When handling fresh chilies, do not touch your face or eyes since painful burning can occur.